The Best Sermon Ever

A study through Jesus' Sermon on the Mount

by

John C. Markum

Copyright © 2023 by John Markum, Santa Clara, CA.

All rights reserved.

No portion of this book may be reproduced in any form without written permission from the publisher or author, except as permitted by U.S. copyright law.

Unless otherwise indicated, Scripture quotations taken from the (NASB®) New American Standard Bible®, Copyright © 1960, 1971, 1977, 1995, 2020 by The Lockman Foundation. Used by permission. All rights reserved. www.lockman.org

The Best Sermon Ever:
A study through Jesus' Sermon on the Mount

TABLE OF CONTENTS

Welcome and Introduction	3
Chapter 1: A Place Called Blessed (5:1-12)	4
Chapter 2: A Path Called Righteous (5:13-20)	8
Chapter 3: A Problem Called Sin (5:21-48)	14
Chapter 4: A Process Called Discipline (6:1-24)	21
Chapter 5: A Poison Called Anxiety (6:24-34)	26
Chapter 6: A Predicament Called Judging (7:1-12)	30
Chapter 7: A Predator Called Imposter (7:13-23)	35
Chapter 8: A Promise Called Security (7:24-28)	39
Memory Verses	43

Welcome and Introduction

Matthew is a peculiar writer with a unique focus into the life and person of Jesus. As one of his original 12 disciples, Matthew offers us a very detailed, firsthand eye-witness report of Christ, particularly on His teachings. More so than the other three Gospel writers, Matthew focuses on **what Jesus said**, and this study reveals this. While much of the content of Jesus' famous Sermon on the Mount is found in the other three Gospels, only Matthew records this as a singular, cohesive sermon. As such, there is a continuity of thought which this study guide attempts to navigate.

Matthew's Gospel is written to a Jewish audience, to reveal to them that Jesus is in fact, their long-awaited Messiah. This doesn't mean that non-Jews cannot learn or appreciate the Sermon on the Mount, nor does it mean that it is not for us. But it does shape how we understand and apply it to our lives. In this sermon, Jesus is revealed as the new and better Lawgiver, and the fulfillment of all the Old Testament. He is shown to care for our suffering in this life, yet teaches us to live for the eternal.

Most importantly, He describes what it means to be citizens of the Kingdom of Heaven. He tells us how to *enter* the Kingdom, and how to *live* as citizens of Heaven, even while we are residents of earth.

To love Jesus is to love His words, and it is sincerely my prayer that you fall deeper in love with Him and His teachings as you walk through this sermon. I designed this Bible study to be most beneficial in the context of a small group. But whether you're participating alone, with a significant other, in a group, or with your entire church family, it blesses my soul that any insight God has given me into His Word could be useful to you. So thank you, for using this book. It is my honor and privilege to follow Jesus with you.

Blessings,

John

Chapter 1: A Place Called *Blessed*

Matthew 5:1-12

I just want my kids to be… *happy*.

But what does that even mean? Kids who are given everything they want are not *happy*, they're *spoiled*. Spoiled kids turn out selfish and complacent… not *happy*. I don't want my kids to "just" be happy – far more importantly, I want them to be *good* men and women. I know that if they are good, it will lead to their *ultimate* happiness – a life worth living.

If we're not careful, we'll often project our spoiled human attitudes and expectations onto God. *If I just want my kids to be happy, why doesn't my Heavenly Father want the same for me?* God doesn't want his children to "just" be happy, He wants us to walk in His ways. And His ways may not make us <u>*immediately*</u> happy, but even better, they will lead to our <u>*ultimate*</u> happiness.

This is how Jesus begins His Sermon on the Mount, with a mind-bending take on what God's idea of happiness looks like for us. It has nothing to do with immediate gratification, and everything to do with eternal blessings. God's idea of happiness is higher than our idea of happiness, it's a place called *Blessed*. And we generally refer to this opening to Jesus' Sermon on the Mount as the "Beatitudes".

Matthew 5:1-12,

"Now when Jesus saw the crowds, He went up on the mountain; and after He sat down, His disciples came to Him. ² And He opened His mouth and began to teach them, saying,

³ "Blessed are the poor in spirit, for theirs is the kingdom of heaven.

⁴ "Blessed are those who mourn, for they will be comforted.

⁵ "Blessed are the gentle, for they will inherit the earth.

⁶ "Blessed are those who hunger and thirst for righteousness, for they will be satisfied.

⁷ "Blessed are the merciful, for they will receive mercy.

⁸ "Blessed are the pure in heart, for they will see God.

⁹ "Blessed are the peacemakers, for they will be called sons of God.

¹⁰ "Blessed are those who have been persecuted for the sake of righteousness, for theirs is the kingdom of heaven.

¹¹ "Blessed are you when people insult you and persecute you, and falsely say all kinds of evil against you because of Me. ¹² Rejoice and be glad, for your reward in heaven is great; for in this same way they persecuted the prophets who were before you."

Redefine Happiness

Nine times in these 12 short verses, Jesus declares, "Blessed are..." to nine different groups of people that we would not normally consider very *"#blessed"*. The Greek word here is *makarios* which means "blessed, happy, to be envied[1]". Let's review the list that Jesus calls blessed and decide whether we would "envy" those in these positions...

- The *poor in spirit* (discouraged, depressed).
- Those who *mourn*.
- The *gentle* (meek).
- Those who *hunger and thirst for righteousness* (justice).
- The *merciful* (forgiving).
- The *pure in heart* (innocent, naïve).
- The *peacemakers* (mediators).
- Those suffering *slander, persecution, and insults*.

If most of these don't sound particularly exciting, you're not alone. Most of us don't want most of these. But what these "Beatitudes" lack in *appeal* they make up for in *familiarity*. Like the original audience hearing this, most of us can *relate* to several of these virtues, even if we don't *desire* them. Today, in any given church, sits a congregation full of people who have been broken in spirit, mourned the loss of a loved one, have felt timid, longed for justice, needed to forgive wrongs done to them, and so on.

Perhaps much of this describes *you*. And you haven't thought of yourself as "blessed" for any of these. And you would be normal for that! But like so many other things in God's Kingdom, as well as here in Jesus' Sermon on the Mount, things tend to operate upside down from our usual perspective.

One of the problems in the world today is *that we often use the same* vocabularies, *but different* dictionaries. What we call mourning, Jesus calls blessed... "to be envied". What we call *struggling*, Jesus calls *favored*.

We need to change our definitions to see ourselves through the eyes of Jesus.

Rethink Your Struggle

There's much more than meets the eye to the *Beatitudes*. If we're not careful and stop here, we may walk away from the text with the idea that Jesus is telling us to "suck it up" and just choose happiness (if that's even a choice) in our otherwise undesirable circumstances. But Jesus doesn't just tell us to <u>be</u> blessed. He tells us that we <u>are</u> blessed and gives us a reason for each.

---

[1] Strong, James. Strong's Greek Concordance: 3107.

Each of these *Beatitudes* is written in the form of Hebrew poetry called, *parallelism*, and they flow in the format of an if/then programming command. For example,

>IF "*poor in spirit*" IS TRUE
>>THEN "*theirs is the Kingdom of Heaven*" IS TRUE
>>RESULT = "BLESSED"

This means that God keeps His word when He says, "The Lord is near to the brokenhearted, and saves those who are crushed in spirit." (Psalm 34:18). **We're blessed because God never asks for more than He gives**. As Paul would go on to write, "our momentary, light affliction is producing for us an eternal weight of glory far beyond all comparison…" (2 Corinthians 4:17). It's not that God is *trivializing* our struggles, but rather that He will *overcompensate* for them. *That* is why He calls us "*blessed*".

Jesus doesn't tell us to "suck it up" when things stink. He offers us hope. Specific hope. He tells us that we are *blessed*, and then tells us *why*. This opening to the Sermon on the Mount gives us hope because our struggle on earth is seen in Heaven.

Rejoice in Your Reward

Verses 11-12 are without question the crescendo to this sermon intro. It intensifies in three ways: the *person*, the *struggle*, and the *blessing* given for the struggle. First, **Jesus gets much more _personal_**. Notice the shift in the subject. He goes from describing "those who" are poor in spirit, mourn, etc. to "you." In verse 11 Jesus changes from addressing people in the third person to the second person. This is more direct to His listeners, then and now.

"Blessed are **_you_** when people insult **_you_** and persecute **_you_**, and falsely say all kinds of evil against **_you_** because of Me." (Matthew 5:11, emphasis mine).

The _struggle_ Jesus describes also intensifies. More than being poor in spirit, or meek, Jesus describes us as "blessed" when we are persecuted, insulted, and lied about. This should certainly invoke a sense of ominous danger in all who are paying attention. But notice that He is not simply referring to any persecution or slander.

The reason He anticipates our persecution is **because we follow Him**. This is the main hook in the rest of His Sermon on the Mount. The entire sermon is built around what it means to follow Jesus, and here, in the intro to the sermon, He sets this up by calling us "blessed" when we suffer mistreatment because of Christ.

Finally, **the _blessing_ given to us intensifies**. Verse 12, "Rejoice and be glad, for your reward in heaven is great; for in this same way they persecuted the prophets who were before you." He tells us to "rejoice and be glad" because our Heavenly Father will reward us greatly when we have suffered in the name of Jesus. The clear implication here is that there is far more to anticipate *after* this life than *during* it. And how we live *now* affects what to expect *then*.

Summary

Jesus begins His Sermon on the Mount by describing His perspective on being blessed. While it's not what we would expect or even desire, Jesus promises that it is worth it in light of eternity. He builds to the point of focusing on our suffering for Him, and the rest of the Sermon on the Mount will teach us what it means to live in His ways.

We need to change our definitions to see ourselves through the eyes of Jesus.

We're blessed because God never asks for more than He gives.

Our life becomes blessed when we allow God to determine our happiness.

Reflection Questions

Which of the Beatitudes do you relate to the most? Why? _____

_____

_____

How have you seen God's blessing in an area others might not consider "good"?

_____

_____

Describe an experience where God "overcompensated" giving back something He asked of you.

_____

_____

How will you change your perspective on your struggles this week?

_____

_____

Chapter 2: A Path Called *Righteous*

Matthew 5:13-20

In Chapter 1, we took a fresh look at what Jesus describes as being blessed, or literally "happy". And we discussed how happiness from God's perspective isn't usually the same as our own ideas of happiness – and yet, God's ways are better. We're not just blessed when things go as we would have them, we are blessed when we suffer, when we hunger, when we yearn for justice.

We also learned that *everything* in God's Kingdom is backward…

- Give, and it will be given to you.
- To save your life, lay it down.
- When you suffer for Me (Jesus), you are *blessed*.

As Jesus completes this thought focusing on the blessing and reward that comes from suffering for the name of Jesus, He continues to turn the focus on us, and what it means to walk with Him. As discussed in the last chapter, the rest of the Sermon on the Mount is focused on what it means to follow Jesus, and He dives straight into that main point by keeping the personal focus on His listeners.

Matthew 5:13-20

[13] "You are the salt of the earth; but if the salt has become tasteless, how can it be made salty again? It is no longer good for anything, except to be thrown out and trampled underfoot by people.

[14] "You are the light of the world. A city set on a hill cannot be hidden; [15] nor do people light a lamp and put it under a basket, but on the lampstand, and it gives light to all who are in the house. [16] Your light must shine before people in such a way that they may see your good works, and glorify your Father who is in heaven.

[17] "Do not presume that I came to abolish the Law or the Prophets; I did not come to abolish, but to fulfill. [18] For truly I say to you, until heaven and earth pass away, not the smallest letter or stroke of a letter shall pass from the Law, until all is accomplished! [19] Therefore, whoever nullifies one of the least of these commandments, and teaches others to do the same, shall be called least in the kingdom of heaven; but whoever keeps and teaches them, he shall be called great in the kingdom of heaven.

[20] "For I say to you that unless your righteousness far surpasses that of the scribes and Pharisees, you will not enter the kingdom of heaven."

Our Righteousness Shows God's Glory

On the heels of being told to rejoice in persecution, Jesus commands His audience to do good deeds, to make the world a better place. He calls us the "salt of the earth" and "light of the world." Let's examine both briefly.

Salt had a number of applications in first-century Israel. Among them, salt served as a flavoring agent (obviously), but also as a preservative. You could even dry-brine meats in salt to add flavor, and preserve their edible shelf life, before the advent of refrigeration. As painful as it may sound, salt could also be diluted, or mixed with other medicinal components to create a healing salve for wounds. Salt was also a rather rare commodity. So much so, that Roman soldiers were often paid in salt. This practice eventually gave way to our modern term "salary".

In summary, being the "salt of the earth" meant that Jesus' followers:

- Add flavor and entice an appetite for more.
- Preserve the world from moral decay.
- Apply healing to a hurting world.
- Add value everywhere we go.

But there is a catch. Salt that isn't salty... isn't really salt. Like mixing up the salt for the sugar, *similarity* does not equal *identity*. And if the "salt" is somehow "not salty" it loses its purpose and value as salt. It cannot flavor, preserve, or heal anything. And it certainly adds no value. As such, it would be pointless to carry it in your inventory or storage. What does one do? We would toss it out. The "trampling underfoot by people" in verse 13 is less about people persecuting Christians as we saw in verses 11-12 earlier. This "trampling" is more of a coincidence. People are not going out of their way to step on the "salt". They're doing so without even realizing it.

In other words, Christians who are not "salty" are irrelevant, because there is no difference between us and our terrestrial environment. The very thing that makes us different from the world, makes us useful to it and the Kingdom of God. You don't season oatmeal with more oatmeal. You don't preserve meat by adding more meat. Likewise, we don't change the world by imitating it, but rather by imitating Christ.

Then there's the light. In Jesus' example, this would been a candle or perhaps a torch. At night, this light could be visible for miles, giving us the mental picture of a lit city on a hill that Jesus references here. Similarly, in the home, a single candle could illuminate an entire room. As followers of Jesus, we bring clarity and certainty in a dark world that is otherwise groping in the dark for truth. We offer hope and safety to weary travelers searching for refuge at night.

Withholding or hiding the very light we are created by God to share is as illogical as putting a basket over a candle. It would only take a minute for the basket to catch fire. Similarly, if we are truly in Christ, our light aches to shine, and will burn inside of us to radiate the light of Jesus. This comment by Jesus reminds us of His description in John 1, "In Him [Jesus] was life, and that life was the light of all mankind. The light shines in the darkness, and the darkness has not overcome it." (John 1:4-5).

The life of Christ inside us, is the same light shining through us.

And as others see the light of Christ inside of us, many will "glorify our Father in Heaven". This is the point of us shining the light of Jesus – so that others may know Him.

Christ is Our Righteousness

This brings us to a shift Jesus makes in the sermon, and we see Him here continuing to point us further toward Himself. But to follow Jesus, we must have some idea of why we need to follow Him. He tells us that He did not come to destroy the Old Testament Law or the Prophets, "but to fulfill" them. That is an interesting thing to say, which no rabbi, prophet, or teacher would have dared claim before or even after Christ.

To "fulfill" the Law meant that Jesus perfectly kept all the commands of God to the nation of Israel. **This speaks of Jesus' righteousness**. While there were certainly many "good" Jews whom the Scriptures called *righteous*, none of them are called *sinless*. King David – a man after God's own heart – committed murder and adultery. Abraham – the founding father of the Jewish nation, who "believed God" and it was accounted to him as righteousness – essentially prostituted his own wife for his safety (Genesis 12:10-20). Each and every prophet from Daniel to Isaiah has instances of admitting their own guilt, sin, and shame. But Jesus is always found blameless.

To fulfill the Prophets meant that Jesus was the long-awaited Messiah, that Israel was looking forward to. Regrettably, they were looking for a political Savior to free them from Roman oppression. But Jesus came for a far greater purpose – to free them from spiritual slavery to sin. This spiritual slavery is more than an earthly inconvenience, it separates eternally from God. This is the oppression that Jesus came to undo through His righteousness.

So to say that Jesus came to "fulfill the Law and the Prophets" means that He is everything that holiness and righteousness are supposed to be. He succeeds where we fail. Jesus concludes this idea by declaring, "For truly I say to you, until heaven and earth pass away, not the smallest letter or stroke of a letter shall pass from the Law, until all is accomplished!" Israel – and all humanity, for that matter – had proven their inability to keep God's laws on their own effort. And Jesus makes clear in verse 19 that the Law of God is not the problem, *we are*.

How Good is "Good Enough"?

And as if that wasn't tough enough, Jesus plays the comparison game, but not in any way we might have expected. Verse 20, "For I say to you that unless your righteousness ***far surpasses that of the scribes and Pharisees***, you will not enter the kingdom of heaven."

(emphasis mine). The Pharisees were proud and self-righteous, but from all outward observations, they were the most "righteous" people Jesus' audience knew besides Him! And if their righteousness wasn't enough, then who's is?!

This statement by Jesus is reminiscent of the words from the prophet Isaiah who says, "We have all become like one who is unclean, and all our righteous deeds are like a polluted garment." (Isaiah 64:6). The phrase "polluted garments" is an English euphemism for the true meaning of the phrase in Hebrew, which I'll allow you to look up on your own, if you're curious enough. Let's just say, "soiled clothes" to make the point. But seriously? If the Pharisees' righteousness isn't good enough, and all our righteous deeds before God are "soiled clothes", how can we do any better? How do we have a meaningful relationship with God we are woefully inadequate to approach?

The problem is not that God doesn't care about our good deeds. It's that our good deeds apart from God make no difference in our sinful state. **We must have a *new* righteousness that is "unsoiled" by our sin.** And that kind of righteousness *does* exist, because of Jesus.

2 Corinthians 5:21, "For our sake, He [God the Father] made Him [Jesus] to be sin who knew no sin, so that in Him ***we might become the righteousness of God***."

Philippians 3:7-9, "But whatever things were gain to me, those things I have counted as loss for the sake of Christ. More than that, I count all things to be loss in view of the surpassing value of knowing Christ Jesus my Lord, for whom I have suffered the loss of all things, and count them but rubbish so that I may gain Christ, and may be found in Him***, not having a righteousness of my own derived from the Law, but that which is through faith in Christ, the righteousness which comes from God on the basis of faith***." (emphasis mine)

Not to overdo the "filth" references, but in the verse above (Philippians 3:8), where Paul says everything he's done in his life apart from Christ as "rubbish", he means... well again, "soiled clothes". The reason I bring this up here again is not from a middle schooler's sense of humor, but to make a driving point clear from Jesus' teaching here in Matthew 5. Our best efforts at "righteousness" apart from Jesus are not just worthless, it's undesirable. I "don't want" to mow the lawn, so I'll tolerate the growing grass a little longer. But "soiled clothes" in my house is something I will actively deal with immediately. It's not just *undesired*, it's *unwelcome*.

Until we see our human effort at righteousness as unwelcome apart from Jesus, we will never be receptive to the righteousness of Jesus that comes by faith in Him. We will continue to brag about our soiled clothes. And that may seem impressive when compared to other people's collections of soiled clothes, but it is unwelcome before God. To approach God, to have access to Heaven, to receive eternal life, we must have a righteousness that far exceeds that of any other human we can compare ourselves with. **We *must* have the righteousness of Christ.**

It can be difficult to accept the truth about our own righteous efforts. We're not alone – the crowds of Jesus' day did also. Especially the Pharisees He just called out! In the next chapter, we'll look closely at the six examples Jesus gives to reveal the true limitations of our righteousness.

Reflection Questions

Why does God seem dissatisfied with our efforts of righteousness?

_____

_____

How do you think the crowd responded to Jesus saying their righteousness must "far surpass" that of the scribes and Pharisees? _____

_____

How do you think people respond *today* to being told their "righteous deeds" are inadequate to God? _____

_____

Have you personally received the "righteousness which comes from God on the basis of faith" in Jesus (Philippians 3:9)?

_____

_____

RECEIVE THE RIGHTEOUSNESS OF CHRIST

Maybe the idea of our righteousness being inadequate is a new concept to you. Most people think God will have a scale in Heaven and weigh our "righteous deeds" on one side, and our unrighteous deeds on the other. And as long as our *good* outweighs the *bad*, we're in, right? The problem is that God doesn't have a scale. God has one standard, and that standard is perfection. We all fall short of that standard, which is why we need the righteousness of Jesus.

The Bible says in Romans 3:23, "For all have sinned and fall short of the glory of God." And later in Romans 6:23, "For the wages of sin is death, but the free gift of God is eternal life in Christ Jesus our Lord." This "eternal life" is because God loved us and sent Christ to die on the cross for our unrighteousness, in order to give us His righteousness. Romans 5:8, "But God demonstrates His own love toward us, in that while we were still sinners, Christ died for us."

To receive this free gift of eternal life, that Jesus died and rose again from the grace to make available to you, all you must do is receive His eternal life for your sinful life. Romans 10:9-11, "that if you confess with your mouth Jesus as Lord, and believe in your heart that God raised Him from the dead, you will be saved; ¹⁰ for with the heart a person believes, **resulting in righteousness**, and with the mouth he confesses, **resulting in salvation**. For the Scripture says, "Whoever believes in Him will not be put to shame." (emphasis mine).

Simply pray to God and acknowledge that you are a sinner separated from God by your sin, and even your own attempts at being righteous. Confess your faith and trust in Jesus' life, death on the cross, and resurrection from the dead. Ask God for the eternal life, which He freely gives to all who will receive it.

And the righteousness and salvation that Jesus offers is yours. Period. "Whoever believes in Him will not be put to shame." And you are a *whoever*! If you're unsure of what to say to God, here's an example, but the most important thing is not the exact words, but the faith to receive God's gift...

God, I come to you today aware of my sin that separates me from You. ***I know there's nothing I can do to save myself from my sin.*** *But* ***I believe in Your Son, Jesus Christ,*** *who died on a cross for my sin, not any sin of His own. And* ***I believe that He rose again to offer me eternal life.*** ***God, I receive this gift right now,*** *and ask you to fill my life with His righteousness and eternal life. God, give me a home in Heaven with you because of what Jesus did for me. And help me to live for You until then. Thank you, God, for saving me from my sin because Jesus died and rose again, so I can be made new in Him. In Jesus' name I pray, Amen.*

Chapter 3: A Problem Called *Sin*

Matthew 5:21-48

In Chapter 2, we discovered the righteous path it takes to get to the Kingdom of God. **This is the theme of Jesus' Sermon on the Mount: <u>entering the Kingdom of God</u>**. In verses 17-20, Jesus reveals that He is the fulfillment of the Law and the Prophets – in other words, our entire Old Testament – and to enter the Kingdom of God, our righteousness must surpass that of the most righteous people the Jews knew: the Pharisees.

But in order for us to receive life in Jesus, we must acknowledge our own deadly path apart from Him. Verse 20 would have jarred the audience. *How can our righteousness "far surpass" that of the most righteous people we can think of?* Jesus goes on to reveal the inadequacies of our human efforts of righteousness with <u>six examples</u> of how our righteousness still falls woefully short of God's righteousness.

Our Better Moses

Jesus presents each of these six examples with a similar "formula". Each time He says something like, "You have heard _____, but I say to you _____." Each of the first "blanks" in the formula is connected to the Laws and teachings of Moses, which Jesus goes on to add to – an extremely taboo move in Jewish culture. To add to the Law was heresy and blasphemy. **No man should dare be so audacious or foolish to think they could add to God's Word... unless it were God Himself.**

It's important to remember that Matthew's Gospel is written specifically for Jews, who did not see themselves as far from God. After all, they were God's chosen people (Genesis 12:1), and the Messiah was promised through their nation. They had been given Moses and the Law. It was them who had the Prophets, and who had performed the ritual temple sacrifices for dozens of generations, according to the Levitical Law given by Moses. How could they possibly be closer to God? They did not yet understand the separation their daily sin created, and Jesus was about to make them understand it.

The Jews held Moses as one of the most evident figures of God's leadership over their nation. He was *the* Lawgiver, who received the Ten Commandments on Mount Sinai, and wrote the Pentateuch – our first five books of Scripture. But *having* God's Word is not the same as *understanding* it. In the second half of Matthew 5, Jesus illuminates our understanding of the Law by doing something radical by Jewish standards – **He *clarifies* and *improves* the Law of Moses.**

This is often lost in Western culture because we don't understand the immensely high regard that the Jews had for the Law of Moses. To be sure, plenty of rabbis in Jesus' day would elaborate and expound on the Torah (literally, "Law"), but none would ever dare suggest that it wasn't clear enough, or needed improvement for our understanding and obedience. **By doing this, Jesus presents Himself as the** *new* **and** *better* **Moses** – able to give the Laws of God, clarify their historic misinterpretation of older Laws, and call out their hypocrisy to the very Laws they claimed to follow so well. In all of these cases, however, *it is* <u>not</u> *God's Laws that are flawed, but our understanding and application of them.*

Let's look at the six examples Jesus gives to challenge their idea of their self-righteous standing before God. As we do consider the question, *do you think you're a good person?* If so, how would you know? Jesus essentially confronts His Jewish audience with the same dilemma…

Example 1: "You shall not murder."

Matthew 5:21-26,

"You have heard that the ancients were told, 'You shall not murder,' and 'Whoever commits murder shall be answerable to the court.' ²² **But I say to you** that everyone who is angry with his brother shall be answerable to the court; and whoever says to his brother, 'You good-for-nothing,' shall be answerable to the supreme court; and whoever says, 'You fool,' shall be guilty enough to go into the fiery hell. ²³ Therefore, if you are presenting your offering at the altar, and there you remember that your brother has something against you, ²⁴ leave your offering there before the altar and go; first be reconciled to your brother, and then come and present your offering. ²⁵ Come to good terms with your accuser quickly, while you are with him on the way to court, so that your accuser will not hand you over to the judge, and the judge to the officer, and you will not be thrown into prison. ²⁶ Truly I say to you, you will not come out of there until you have paid up the last quadrans." (emphasis added)

When asked, *do you think you're a good person*, and people say, *yes*, murder tends to be the first thing mentioned as an example of our "goodness." If we have never killed someone in cold blood we're at least not as bad as "bad" people, right? Wrong. Jesus begins His examples of our sinful nature by going straight for our favorite scapegoat. Jesus says that if we harbor anger and hatred toward our brother, we shall stand before God under the same judgment as a literal murderer.

How often have we entertained feelings of anger, bitterness, and hatred toward others? If hatred looks to God like murder looks to us, do any of us still have clean hands? Probably not. "You shall not commit murder" is one of the Ten Commandments (Exodus 20:13), and Jesus immediately begins His series of examples by going to the one thing most of us assume we would pass the test on. But there's more…

Example 2: "You shall not commit adultery."

Matthew 5:27-30,

"You have heard that it was said, 'You shall not commit adultery'; [28] **but I say to you** that everyone who looks at a woman with lust for her has already committed adultery with her in his heart. [29] Now if your right eye is causing you to sin, tear it out and throw it away from you; for it is better for you to lose one of the parts of your body, than for your whole body to be thrown into hell. [30] And if your right hand is causing you to sin, cut it off and throw it away from you; for it is better for you to lose one of the parts of your body, than for your whole body to go into hell." (emphasis added)

The murder example was probably the safest place people assume their innocence. Jesus moved from that to the next obvious criteria we assume our innocence: adultery. Again, Jesus corrects our presumption of self-righteousness. We likely don't know anyone who has personally committed murder, but many of us have likely known multiple cheaters. Being free from committing adultery would certainly set us apart, if true (Exodus 20:14).

But here, Jesus addresses our struggle with lusting after others. He tells us that simply entertaining elicit fantasies of others in the privacy of our own minds is exactly why God condemned adultery. **The _sin_ of adultery occurs before the _act_ of adultery**. Jesus goes on to use hyperbole, giving an extreme example to make a serious point: "It is better for you to lose one of the parts of your body than for your whole body to go into Hell." (v. 30). Jesus is not supporting self-mutilation, to be clear, but His point should be obvious, then we must guard ourselves against the thoughts that lead us into sin and separation from God at great cost.

Example 3: Divorce

Matthew 5:31-32,

"Now it was said, 'Whoever sends his wife away is to give her a certificate of divorce'; [32] but I say to you that everyone who divorces his wife, except for the reason of sexual immorality, makes her commit adultery; and whoever marries a divorced woman commits adultery."

Directly following Jesus' teaching on lust and adultery, He adds a thought on marriage and divorce, quoting from Deuteronomy 24:1, where Moses allows for divorce. Jesus actually condemns divorcing our spouse – well, under most circumstances, at least. He tells us that divorce – aside from them committing the act of adultery – is itself an act of adultery. Worse yet, in their time, a divorced woman had very few choices in first-century Israel. Generally, she would either have to remarry or turn to prostitution to support herself. In both circumstances, Jesus calls this adultery, because it violates the vows that were made before God to each other.

Additionally, the man who remarries after divorcing his wife (apart from adulterous reasons), also commits adultery.

Now, misunderstand this: While God *hates* divorce, **He still *loves* divorcees**. And God also loves divorcees who have been remarried, despite how Jesus points out their sin. He would go on in Matthew 19:3-12 to talk about why God loves marriage and seeks to protect it from adultery and divorce. But for this passage, the takeaway is that marriage is a covenant relationship before God that is intended to be a lifelong commitment. Because of this, **it should only be broken under the most extreme circumstances**. And even this should be viewed as a regrettable circumstance. Those who have had to go through a divorce (regardless of the reason) will generally agree that it was one of the worst things they've had to go through.

My wife, Tiffany, and I will also be publishing a new book in 2024 entitled ***The Worthwhile Marriage***, which will walk through the Biblical model of healthy, strong marriages. You can find out more from my website, johnmarkum.org, and even sign up to get notified when it's published, if interested.

Example 4: "You shall not make false vows."

Matthew 5:33-37,

"Again, you have heard that the ancients were told, 'You shall not make false vows, but shall fulfill your vows to the Lord.' **34** But I say to you, take no oath at all, neither by heaven, for it is the throne of God, **35** nor by the earth, for it is the footstool of His feet, nor by Jerusalem, for it is the city of the great King. **36** Nor shall you take an oath by your head, for you cannot make a single hair white or black. **37** But make sure your statement is, 'Yes, yes' or 'No, no'; anything beyond these is of evil origin."

There is a cadence to these six examples Jesus gives. He goes from the most extreme example we think we keep (murder), to the next (adultery), to the breaking of marriage vows (divorce), to the breaking of any vows.

It was common in Jesus' time to qualify your vows ("solemn promise") with spiritual-sounding qualifiers. Jesus gives a few examples in these verses, such as swearing by heaven, earth, the temple, or the hair on their head. But these qualifiers were treated as out-clauses. Like the promise maker had their fingers crossed when they swore to do something!

Jesus calls out this hypocrisy for what it is: bearing false witness, i.e., *lying*. This again violates one of the Ten Commandments, and Jesus instructs His listeners to just do what you said you would do. Let your "Yes" mean "yes", and your "no" mean "no!"

Example 5: "Eye for an eye, and Tooth for a tooth."

Matthew 5:38-41,

"You have heard that it was said, 'Eye for eye, and tooth for tooth.' [39] But I say to you, do not show opposition against an evil person; but whoever slaps you on your right cheek, turn the other toward him also. [40] And if anyone wants to sue you and take your tunic, let him have your cloak also. [41] Whoever forces you to go one mile, go with him two. [42] Give to him who asks of you, and do not turn away from him who wants to borrow from you."

Man, it feels good to get even with someone who has wronged you! What? You know it's true! And to make it better, there was a provision made in the Law of Moses to get even! But there are multiple shifts from the Old Testament to the New Testament. One of those is the focus moving from national identity to individual identity. The command to take an eye for an eye, or a tooth for a tooth was a matter of governance, that individuals would often take into their own hands (Exodus 21:23-25).

Both Jesus and the NT writers affirm the role of government, and our submission to authority, as best as we can while following God's ways. Jesus said, "...render to Caesar the things that are Caesar's; and to God the things that are God's." (Matthew 22:21). Later, Paul writes to the Romans, "Every person is to be in subjection to the governing authorities. For there is no authority except from God, and those which exist are established by God." (Romans 13:1). Government has a role, and that role includes punishing evil. We call this justice. But on an individual level, as Christians, it's called something else: revenge.

Rather, Christ instructs us with three alternatives to being taken advantage of, and they all have unique components.

Getting slapped on the right cheek with the right hand was generally a means of excommunicating someone from the synagogue or temple. By turning the other cheek, you would force the synagogue leader or priest to either slap you with their left hand (which would be demeaning to the one slapping you), or use the back of their hand to slap you (which was equivalent to punching you, making you their equal). This was also a warning that following Jesus would often mean being kicked out of their own synagogues.

When being sued over a dispute, rather than giving the bare minimum demanding, go above and beyond. When taken to task for your tunic (primary garment), offer to give them your cloak (outer layer) as well. This denied them the future opportunity of claiming you have not paid in full, and made you look better before the judge, should they attempt to sue you for more in the future.

And finally, walking an extra mile. It was custom for any Roman soldier to require a subject of Rome to walk with them for up to a mile, carrying their gear for them. This was part of the reason the average soldier was despised by the average commoner. But the soldiers were limited to only asking them to walk a mile, as a means of limiting the expectations of their subjects. By offering to walk an extra mile with the soldier, you would be using generosity as a weapon! It put the soldier in a strange position, because they could get in trouble for even allowing you to walk more than the one-mile limit.

Example 6: "You shall love your neighbor and hate your enemy."

Matthew 5:43-48,

"You have heard that it was said, 'You shall love your neighbor and hate your enemy.' ⁴⁴ But I say to you, love your enemies and pray for those who persecute you, ⁴⁵ so that you may prove yourselves to be sons of your Father who is in heaven; for He causes His sun to rise on the evil and the good, and sends rain on the righteous and the unrighteous. ⁴⁶ For if you love those who love you, what reward do you have? Even the tax collectors, do they not do the same? ⁴⁷ And if you greet only your brothers and sisters, what more are you doing than others? Even the Gentiles, do they not do the same? ⁴⁸ Therefore you shall be perfect, as your heavenly Father is perfect."

This one gives us an example of how we often twist Scripture. Jesus is quoting the culture, which is misquoting the Bible. Leviticus 19:18 says, "You shall not take vengeance or bear a grudge against the sons of your own people, **but you shall love your neighbor as yourself**: I am the Lord." (emphasis added). By the first century, this proverbial command was often stretched to add the "hate your enemies" portion of the quote Jesus cites. Just because God told us to love our neighbor does not mean that we can hate others, including our enemies.

Jesus goes on to point out that even the Gentiles (non-Jews) who did not know the one true God, had the same moral standard. Shouldn't those who know God be better? And doesn't God cause basic blessings, like rain, to fall on their crops just as He does for the Jews?

In Summary

Jesus concludes His six examples much like He began them in verse 20, where He tells them that their righteousness must "far surpass" the scribes and Pharisees. In verse 43 He summarizes, "Therefore you shall be **perfect**, as your heavenly Father is perfect." (emphasis added).

The point of these examples is to show that **holiness is higher than we think**. And yet we are commanded to be perfect "as your Heavenly Father" is perfect. The point of personal holiness is not to limit our pleasure, but to limit our pain, and to draw us into proximity with God.

You may have noticed that several times in these examples, Jesus takes our outward focus and turns it internal. It's far easier to look right on the outside than it is to be right on the inside. We can fool others much easier than we can fool God or ourselves. Psalm 51:6, "Behold, You [God] desire truth in the innermost being."

This creates somewhat of a paradox for Christianity:

- The closer I feel to Jesus, the more aware I become of my sin.
- The more aware I become of my sin, the further I feel from Jesus.

But remember, the point of Jesus' sermon is to draw people to Him, and into His Kingdom. The Gospel literally means "good news". But we cannot respond in faith to the good news, until we understand and accept the bad news – that we are much, much farther from God in our human efforts, than any of us want to believe. Even when we manage to get it right on the outside, we struggle internally with lust, anger, hatred, envy, dishonesty, and more. Jesus alone is the righteousness that allows us forgiveness. <u>His</u> righteousness is required to enter <u>His</u> Kingdom.

Reflection Questions

What are some internal spiritual struggles you have, that most people don't see from the outside? _____

_____

Does it seem more natural to judge others from the outside, or feel insecure when you compare yourself to others? Why? _____

_____

Why do you think God cares about our internal thoughts if we're "mostly" good on the outside?
_____

_____

Is it possible for us to be "perfect" as our Heavenly Father is? Explain…
_____

_____

_____

Chapter 4: A Process Called *Discipline*

Matthew 6:1-24

As we close Matthew 5, we may have a sense of heaviness. We just learned that we must be more righteous than humanly possible to enter the Kingdom of God, and that our internal thought life is just as incriminating of our sin as our outward actions. But Jesus' Sermon on the Mount is not intended to guilt us, as much as it is to convict us. There's an important difference. Guilt and shame are the result of being aware of our sin, but conviction is agreeing that our sin is a problem and committing to doing something about it. In Matthew 6, Jesus takes us from feeling bad about our sin, to giving us useful direction toward living in God's ways – inward and outward.

Matthew 6:1-24

"Take care not to practice your righteousness in the sight of people, to be noticed by them; otherwise you have no reward with your Father who is in heaven. **2** "So when you give to the poor, do not sound a trumpet before you, as the hypocrites do in the synagogues and on the streets, so that they will be praised by people. Truly I say to you, they have their reward in full. **3** But when you give to the poor, do not let your left hand know what your right hand is doing, **4** so that your charitable giving will be in secret; and your Father who sees what is done in secret will reward you. **5** "And when you pray, you are not to be like the hypocrites; for they love to stand and pray in the synagogues and on the street corners so that they will be seen by people. Truly I say to you, they have their reward in full. **6** But as for you, when you pray, go into your inner room, close your door, and pray to your Father who is in secret; and your Father who sees what is done in secret will reward you.

7 "And when you are praying, do not use thoughtless repetition as the Gentiles do, for they think that they will be heard because of their many words. **8** So do not be like them; for your Father knows what you need before you ask Him.

9 "Pray, then, in this way:

> 'Our Father, who is in heaven, Hallowed be Your name. **10** Your kingdom come. Your will be done, on earth as it is in heaven. **11** Give us this day our daily bread. **12** And forgive us our debts, as we also have forgiven our debtors. **13** And do not lead us into temptation, but deliver us from evil.' **14** For if you forgive other people for their offenses, your heavenly Father will also forgive you. **15** But if you do not forgive other people, then your Father will not forgive your offenses.

16 "Now whenever you fast, do not make a gloomy face as the hypocrites do, for they distort their faces so that they will be noticed by people when they are fasting. Truly I say to you, they have their reward in full. **¹⁷** But as for you, when you fast, anoint your head and wash your face, **¹⁸** so that your fasting will not be noticed by people but by your Father who is in secret; and your Father who sees what is done in secret will reward you.

As we review these verses, Jesus gives us three positive examples of how His followers are to live. Let's review those three below...

Others not Self

In verses 1-4, Jesus sets the tone of our lives by discussing the nature of our generosity, particularly toward the poor, or "alms" giving. Apparently from these verses, the wealthy and religious leaders would throw a literal parade when making their tithe donations to the local synagogue. They would similarly make sure people also noticed them when giving alms for the poor. It's the equivalent of giving money to a homeless person but making sure to post a selfie to social media of you helping them out. We know that when we see someone do this we wonder, *Was this about you or them?*

If you've ever thought that you're not alone. Jesus feels the same way! He clearly wants us to be generous, but He wants to be the one to bless us for our generosity, rather than us seek it from others. For giving to the needy privately, "your Father who sees what is done in secret will reward you." (v. 4).

Jesus wants His followers – the people who will enter His Kingdom – to do good for others, not ourselves. Mark 10:45, "For the Son of Man did not come to be served, but to serve, and to give His life as a ransom for many." When we serve others through our acts of love and generosity, and do so out of sincere care for them rather than ourselves; we are living by the very same virtues as the One we say has saved us.

God's Attention, not People's Approval

After the matter of giving privately rather than publicly, Jesus tells us the Father will reward us for doing so. He then moves into the second example His followers should live by; **God's attention, not people's approval**. And He does so by telling us two things not to do: Pray for people's approval, and repetitively recite words (v. 5-15).

Rather, Jesus admonishes us to pray privately – much like our giving habits. It is here that He gives us what is commonly known as "The Lord's Prayer". I submit that this is better titled "The Lord's *Model* Prayer" as this prayer does not apply to Jesus praying. That's in John 17, and worth the time studying. Rather, Jesus showing us how to pray. Not *what* to pray... This example of prayer, powerful as it is, was not intended to be vainly recited over and over again as some church traditions do. Jesus literally said not to do that two verses earlier! Instead, He says to pray *like* this…

- *"Our Father, who is in Heaven"*. He is our Father – personal, yet holy in Heaven.
- *"Hallowed be Your name"*. We address God with reverence and worship.
- *"Your Kingdom come, Your will be done, on earth as it is in Heaven."* Rather than beginning to pray and ask God for what we want, we submit ourselves to what He wants.
- *"Give us this day our daily bread."* We seek provision from God for our real needs.
- *"Forgive us our debts."* We acknowledge our sins and seek forgiveness.
- *"…as we forgive our debtors."* Recognize our need to forgive others as well.
- *"Do not lead us into temptation, but deliver us from evil."* Seek guidance from Him.
- **"For yours is the Kingdom, and the power, and the glory forever. Amen."* End with reverence, and worship, like the beginning.

* (*Earliest known manuscripts of the NT are missing this phrase, but it is often considered canon to this passage, though it may have actually been written in later. This does not mean it does not belong in our Bibles, though some translations omit it*).

For maintaining a private, personal prayer life with God, Jesus again affirms, "Pray to your Father who is in secret; and your Father who sees what is done in secret will reward you." (v. 6).

Power from on High, not Popularity Here Below

Last of all, Jesus addresses the discipline of fasting in verses 16-18. His beginning instruction to us about fasting is "*When* you fast…" This of course implies that we are fasting in the first place. In Jesus' day, there was a problem with very pious Pharisees wearing old clothes, not shaving or showering, and walking around looking miserable so everyone knew they were fasting and could admire how spiritual they were. By contrast, in 21st-century America, we get "hangry" when we haven't had a mid-afternoon snack between lunch and dinner! But fasting is a critical discipline to the life of a believer.

Fasting is the intentional denying ourselves, for a specific period of time, in order to draw closer to God and seek His wisdom and strength.

My wife, Tiffany, and I try to go on regular date nights. When we go to various restaurants, I know that there are certain places we *cannot* sit. As a high extrovert, I tend to make new friends everywhere I go. And normally this isn't a problem. But when we're out on a date, my attention should be on her, not making new friends.

Similarly, when we fast, we are supposed to do so for *intimacy* with God, not *admiration* of others. Fasting is powerful. Some of my deepest, most enriching moments with God have been through fasting. And if we're not careful, we can spend our whole lives trying to impress strangers rather than grow closer to the One who redeemed us. Fasting is the discipline of voluntarily walking through the truth of Paul's statement in 2 Corinthians 12, "For when I am weak, then I am strong." (v. 10). Paul had learned through his own circumstances that God's strength in my weakness was far greater than my strength without God.

When we fast, we acknowledge that we *must* eat eventually. But right now, for this day (or week, etc.), being with God is more important than my next meal. We're living the words of Jesus after he had fasted just before His Sermon on the Mount in Matthew 4:4, "Man shall not live on bread alone, but on every word that comes out of the mouth of God."

As Jesus concludes this third example, again He says, "Your Father who sees what is done in secret will reward you." Three times, we're told to do our good deeds for God's glory not our own. And that doing so will result in God's blessing on us, rather than people's. And God is a much better "blesser"!

What Does This Mean?

There is plenty of continuity of thought from the six examples of our internal sin struggles from Matthew 5 and the three examples here of how to walk as followers of Jesus. Two of them to consider are...

1. **God cares more about what I'm <u>becoming</u> than just what I'm <u>doing</u>, the same is true – not just of our sin/temptation - but of our good deeds also. And,**
2. **You can go through the right motions without having the right emotions.**

Verses 19-24 are often treated as unrelated to these three disciples of giving, praying, and fasting. But consider that all three times Jesus promises us a reward from our Heavenly Father. He then goes to summarize our perspective:

"***Do not store up for yourselves treasures on earth***, where moth and rust destroy, and where thieves break in and steal. ²⁰ ***But store up for yourselves treasures in heaven***, where neither moth nor rust destroys, and where thieves do not break in or steal; ²¹ ***for where your treasure is, there your heart will be also.***" (Matthew 6:19-21, emphasis mine)

The point Jesus is making in all three of these disciplines is to live for the Kingdom of God, not the Kingdom of Man. This is right back to the "big idea" for Jesus' Sermon on the Mount in the first place. And this passage and these disciplines help us understand **how to live as *citizens* of the Kingdom of God, while being *residents* in the kingdoms of men.**

Reflection Questions

The assumption to all three of these disciplines is that we're doing them. Which one of the three do you struggle with doing the most? Why? _____

_____

_____

What do we gain from having these private disciplines? What are some examples you can think of, how God "rewards" us? _____

_____

Why do we need to keep our focus on Heaven while we're still living here below?

_____

_____

Do you see Christians as struggling to serve God rather than wealth (v. 24)? What about yourself? _____

_____

_____

Chapter 5: A Poison Called *Anxiety*

Matthew 6:24-34

Do you remember the first day of the Covid-19 pandemic? I'll never forget it! Those first few days were pure chaos, as people, preachers, and politicians all tried to discern what we were supposed to say and do. I remember watching the local news as San Francisco Mayor London Breed gave a speech to the residents of the city. I don't remember how many times she actually said it, but I remember at least five times that she said, "Don't panic!" in her address. Now, I don't care what your political beliefs are, but anytime any politician says "Don't panic" that many times, I kind of start to panic!

Any husband who has told his upset wife to "calm down" knows how useless – and counterproductive – those words are, without any substance. If you want your wife to relax, you have to give her a reason to do so, not attempt to *tell* her to do so!

Why *is more important than* what.

Telling people what to do may or may not work. But if we understand the *why*, then we tend to be more motivated to follow the *what*. Jesus knew this better than anyone. Having just called us to spiritual disciplines that engage the heart not just the hands, He reassures us that God is in control, even when things in our lives seem out of control.

Matthew 6:24-34
"No one can serve two masters; for either he will hate the one and love the other, or he will be devoted to one and despise the other. You cannot serve God and wealth.

[25] For this reason I say to you, do not be worried about your life, as to what you will eat or what you will drink; nor for your body, as to what you will put on. Is life not more than food, and the body more than clothing? [26] Look at the birds of the sky, that they do not sow, nor reap, nor gather crops into barns, and yet your heavenly Father feeds them. Are you not much more important than they? [27] And which of you by worrying can add a single day to his life's span? [28] And why are you worried about clothing? Notice how the lilies of the field grow; they do not labor nor do they spin thread for cloth, [29] yet I say to you that not even Solomon in all his glory clothed himself like one of these. [30] But if God so clothes the grass of the field, which is alive today and tomorrow is thrown into the furnace, will He not much more clothe you? You of little faith! [31] Do not worry then, saying, 'What are we to eat?' or 'What are we to drink?' or 'What are we to wear for clothing?' [32] For the Gentiles eagerly seek all these things; for your heavenly Father knows that you need all these things. [33] But seek first His kingdom and His righteousness, and all these things will be provided to you.

[34] "So do not worry about tomorrow; for tomorrow will worry about itself. Each day has enough trouble of its own."

Let's examine Jesus' instructions on anxiety and how we overcome it.

1. Recognize that worry is a cruel master.

Jesus begins this segment of the Sermon on the Mount referencing what He previously said about us not being able to serve two masters (v. 24). In verse 25 He begins with, "For this reason". In other words, "*Since you can't serve two masters*, do not worry about your life…". This means we have a choice about where our focus is going to be occupied: we can focus on God and His goodness, <u>or</u> we can focus on the worries of this world. **But we can't do both**.

Later in Matthew 14, Jesus would come walking to the disciples on the water. Understanding that there was a relationship between what Jesus commands and what he could do, Peter asks Jesus to command him onto the water (Matthew 14:28). Jesus tells him to come, and true to the test, Peter is able to do as Jesus commanded him. But Peter recognized that the waves were still boisterous, and the wind was still blowing wildly. As he began to focus on the chaos around him, he began to turn his attention off Jesus. Consequentially, he began to sink, called out for help, and Jesus rescued him.

Similarly, we can only focus on one thing at a time. And what we focus on gets bigger in our perspective. The brain makes the things our mind focuses on appear bigger and more important. As a result, when we focus on the worries of this world, they seem much bigger and more important than they actually are. We operate in this world of chaos and anxiety all the time. Some of us (me!) even lie to ourselves and try convincing ourselves and others that we thrive under pressure… yeah, that sounds healthy! **That feeling of "thriving" in chaos is actually a sign of *addiction*.** All sin is addictive. The rush we get by bouncing from one chaotic obstacle to the next is the same description of a substance abuser managing their cravings from one hit to the next.

This is why worry is a cruel master. We think we're in control of it, but it grabs our minds and demands its way. And telling ourselves to "not worry" is like the politicians saying, "Don't panic". It just doesn't work. We must have a new focus, otherwise, we'll always come back for another hit of anxiety. We must begin by acknowledging the anxious thoughts of our hearts, but fortunately, Jesus doesn't leave us on "don't worry," but provides actual substance to the command.

2. Believe your Heavenly Father knows your needs.

Jesus gives us two examples after telling us to not worry: birds and lilies. He points out how the birds do not plant gardens or store harvests, yet God feeds them, and knows when something happens to each one. He also adorns the lilies in beauty incomparable to even the lavish King Solomon. The rhetorical question Jesus asks, "Are you not much more than they?" highlights God's awareness of our needs, just like His awareness of the birds.

But trusting God doesn't mean we sit back and do nothing since God will provide. It means that we operate in cooperation with God. **God's greatest desire for us is that we walk with Him**, and experience life through an ongoing relationship with Him. My father would read this text and point out that God does in fact provide food for the birds, but He doesn't throw it in their nest. They still must go out and find the food. Similarly, trusting God doesn't mean we *don't* work, but rather that we do work, *because* we trust He will provide.

In verse 32, He tells us that the Gentiles (non-Jews, i.e., those who did not know the Lord), covet and stress over these basic things. The implication is that we are not to be like them, but to realize that "your heavenly Father knows that you need all these things."

Keep your eyes on <u>Jesus</u>, he already has His eyes on <u>you</u>.

Verses 33-34, Jesus gives us the focus of our heart's attention rather than our worries and stresses: Himself, and His Kingdom. Remember, the entire Sermon on the Mount is about the Kingdom of God, how to enter it, and live as citizens of it. So this ties straight into the central theme of His Sermon.

Because we are incapable of "not worrying" without a new focus, Jesus is directing us to where we should give our attention. Like Peter in Matthew 14, if we keep our eyes on Jesus, we will walk across the storms of life safely. It is worth noting that, like Peter, the storm still rages (more on that in Chapter 8). We are guaranteed to have difficulties in life. Jesus already spoke to this at the beginning of His sermon which we covered in the first chapter.

But the promise of this passage is that the Lord will watch over us, as we keep our lives oriented to His Kingdom and His ways. When we realize this, the focus of our mundane tasks becomes less about paying bills, going to school, and raising families. Instead, we begin to see everything we do through the lens of God's Kingdom. We're not just employees at a company, we're marketplace missionaries of the good news. We're not just parents, we're modeling faithfulness to the next generation. We're not just paying bills and getting by, we're generous stewards of the blessings of God. We're not just going to class, we're equipping ourselves to fulfill the calling God has placed on us.

Summary

The solution to stress is a new focus, and confidence in the One who watches over us. If I seek God's Kingdom and righteousness (which we also unpacked in Chapter 2) He takes care of my needs. Because of this, we maintain our focus on the cross.

Paul also addresses this in Philippians 4:4-8, admonishing us, "Do not be anxious about anything, but in everything by prayer and pleading with thanksgiving, let your requests be made known to God." We already saw that God knows our needs (v. 32), so Paul is telling us that we can express these needs, trusting that God already knows them.

Anxiety is our cue to pray.

When we get stressed and overwhelmed, let it serve as our reminder that God is bigger than our stress. And He is capable of navigating us through our worry if we keep our eyes on Him. For more on Philippians, enjoy the study I created, **Developing Joy**, which walks through the entire book. Paul doesn't just tell the Philippian church to have joy, he shows them how.

Reflection Questions

What are the issues you tend to worry over the most? _____

_____

How do worry and anxiety affect your relationship with God? _____

_____

_____

How will you manage stress and worry this week? _____

_____

_____

What are the things you can focus on today that will be productive and give God glory?

_____

_____

Chapter 6: A Predicament Called *Judging*

Matthew 7:1-12

We live in a world of constant feedback. We send a text and expect a reply in under a minute. Presidential elections used to take us months to determine and share the results. Now we can project the winner in each state and determine the President-elect before all the votes are even completely counted – all on the same night we vote. Even as I've been typing this study guide, my grammar check consistently calls out words I use a lot, which it finds "excessive". Words like *actually*.

Before the 1990's, our access to information was largely dictated by what we experienced, the people we knew, the news we watched, or the books we read. In the age of social media, we can access people around the planet in seconds. Information is everywhere, and frankly, a high percentage of it is *garbage*. While you and I can learn almost anything we want to, we have to weed through a lot of unhelpful information to get the right information.

Today, feedback is not a matter of *collecting* information, but *curating* information.

But even before the internet, we needed to have discernment in how we give and receive feedback. The next portion of Jesus' Sermon on the Mount addresses this with the internet's favorite shame word: *judging*. But let's read Jesus' instructions about giving and taking feedback and understand what He really meant about judging others and being judged.

Matthew 7:1-12
"Do not judge, so that you will not be judged. ² For in the way you judge, you will be judged; and by your standard of measure, it will be measured to you. ³ Why do you look at the speck that is in your brother's eye, but do not notice the log that is in your own eye? ⁴ Or how can you say to your brother, 'Let me take the speck out of your eye,' and look, the log is in your own eye? ⁵ You hypocrite, first take the log out of your own eye, and then you will see clearly to take the speck out of your brother's eye!

⁶ "Do not give what is holy to dogs, and do not throw your pearls before pigs, or they will trample them under their feet, and turn and tear you to pieces.

⁷ "Ask, and it will be given to you; seek, and you will find; knock, and it will be opened to you. ⁸ For everyone who asks receives, and the one who seeks finds, and to the one who knocks it will be opened. ⁹ Or what person is there among you who, when his son asks for a loaf of bread, will give him a stone? ¹⁰ Or if he asks for a fish, he will not give him a snake, will he? ¹¹ So if you, despite being evil, know how to give good gifts to your children, how much more will your Father who is in heaven give good things to those who ask Him!

¹² "In everything, therefore, treat people the same way you want them to treat you, for this is the Law and the Prophets.

To Judge or Not to Judge

Many people – including many Christians – stop at verse 1, declaring that Jesus Himself told us not to judge. But in the verses immediately after that (v. 2-12), He actually instructs us on <u>how</u> to judge one another. So with that in mind, we must ask, *Did Jesus mean something else when He said, "Do not judge, so that you will not be judged"?* Spoiler: Yes.

Jesus was not instructing those who would follow Him to "not judge". For one, it's impossible. You and I make judgments all day every day. The word judge simply means "to discern", and we discern things as good or bad, right or wrong, etc. all the time. And that is good and right to do so. We mistake the word here *judge*, to being synonymous with *condemn*. And from that perspective, sure, we should not condemn people. That is distinctly God's responsibility. But we should judge actions. This is the difference between *approval* and *acceptance*.

Acceptance is implicit in loving others. You cannot love someone while simultaneously rejecting them. So when the Bible tells us that "God so <u>loved</u> the world" (John 3:16), it's consistent when it also says, "<u>Whoever</u> calls upon the name of the Lord shall be saved." (Romans 10:13). **But accepting *people* doesn't mean we approve of all their <u>actions</u>.** In fact, love requires us to judge their actions, in order to be useful to their best interests.

Judging others means we must *lovingly* confront unhealthy behaviors in each other. In every case, the goal is not to condemn them but to deliver them from the actions and attitudes that are unhealthy for them, and their relationship with God or others. We must also avoid trying to conform them to our image, but rather into the image of Christ, and who He has created them to be as a reflection of Himself.

How to *Give* Feedback

Jesus actually gives us instructions for how to correct (judge) one another, so that our lives as Kingdom-citizens honors Him. Verses 2-6 give us the illustration of calling out a speck in someone else's eye, while having an entire log stuck in our own eye. But verse 5 specifically tells us to remove the log from our eye so that we will be able to point the speck out of someone else's eye.

Here is how Jesus instructs us to correct one another:

- **Treat them how you would want to be treated**. Jesus immediately tells us in verse 2 that we will be judged by the same measure that we judge others.
- **Be aware of your own sin**. He warns us to deal with our own log first. Otherwise, we're hypocrites, correcting others while ignoring our own sin.
- **Address your biases**. When we fail to address our sin, we can't see clearly because of the "log" in our eye. This log skews our perspective.
- **Seek restoration, not condemnation**. The goal is for us both to be able to see clearly, not for one of us to be right and the other wrong.
- **Express your support for them**. Sometimes all it takes is reassuring someone, "I am **for** you." Or "I wouldn't bring this up if I didn't care about you."

- **Know when to save your energy**. Not everyone will take feedback well, regardless of how lovingly it's delivered. Not throwing "pearls before pigs" means we don't waste what is precious on those who are committed to rejecting it, or trampling us in the process.

How to *Take* Feedback

Verse 7 is often quoted on its own, without the context of Jesus teaching on correction and giving/receiving feedback. It would seem like a hard shift if Jesus wasn't continuing the same thought. Verse 7, "Ask, and it will be given to you; seek, and you will find; knock, and it will be opened to you." But what is *it* that Jesus is talking about? Correction! Feedback. Discernment. "Judgment". Why in the world would anyone seek that?!

Proverbs 9:7-9, "One who corrects a scoffer gets dishonor for himself, and one who rebukes a wicked person gets insults for himself. Do not rebuke a scoffer, or he will hate you; rebuke a wise person and he will love you. Give instruction to a wise person and he will become still wiser; teach a righteous person and he will increase his insight."

When we compare Matthew 7:6-8 to Proverbs 9:7-9, we see a lot of symmetry. Both Jesus and Solomon (the writer of Proverbs) tell us not to correct those who will reject all feedback (i.e., "pigs", "scoffers"), and they tell us that wise people will not only receive feedback, but they will also seek it. Jesus compares our desire for feedback to that of a father whose son asks for bread or fish. Would a good father give them stones and serpents instead?! So much more, our Heavenly Father will lovingly give us what we need, even when it comes to correction.

We often fear God's "feedback" because we're afraid of being judged ("condemned"). But God's judgment of His children is of discernment, not condemnation. "Therefore there is now **no condemnation** at all for those who are in Christ Jesus." (Romans 8:1, emphasis mine). We do not need to fear God's judgment of us in Christ, because we have already been declared "not guilty" by virtue of Jesus who paid for all our sin on the cross. So the judgment of God to us as Christians is to make us more like Christ, not to shame us for the sin Jesus died to set us free from.

The judgment of God is to *correct* us, not *condemn* us.

And the uncomfortable truth is, God often corrects us through one another. Back to our passage in Proverbs, instruction is given about correcting a wise person. Proverbs 9:9 directly tells us "Give instruction to a wise person and he will become still wiser; teach a righteous person and he will increase his insight." Did you notice the irony of this verse? Receiving correction from others doesn't mean you are not wise, but rejecting healthy feedback means you are not.

Here are some useful tips on receiving feedback from others:

- **Stay humble**. Giving and receiving healthy feedback both require humility on the part of both sides.
- **Ask good clarifying questions**. Seeking feedback means trying to understand what someone else notices about you.

- **Consider their perspective.** Just because they confront you doesn't mean they care for you, or that they understand you. They could have a log in their eye. Your job in receiving feedback is not to find fault in the other person in order to negate their feedback. But you may need to weigh their perspective before taking what they see as "good" feedback.
- **Acknowledge error.** In almost all feedback, there is something to be gained. Again, a wise person can be corrected. Whether you agree with <u>all</u> the feedback, what is being shared that can make you more like Jesus?
- **Thank them.** If a wise person will love the one willing to make them better, we should express gratitude to those who help us do so. "Thank you for having the courage to point this out to me." "Thank you for helping me." "Thank you for bringing this to my attention." These are a few basic examples of how we can receive feedback with love.

In my church, we have a mantra we often quote, that we are "Better Together." And I sincerely believe that as followers of Jesus, we are Kingdom citizens together to make each other better together, and more like Jesus who saved us to Himself. God speaks to us through His Word, His Spirit, and through His family, the church.

We're only better together when we actually make each other better.

Jesus summarizes this point on feedback in verse 12. "In everything, therefore, treat people the same way you want them to treat you, for this is the Law and the Prophets." If you recall, Jesus taught us that He came to "fulfill" the Law and the Prophets back in Matthew 5. Here, He is showing us how we can do so in Him, by treating one another well in giving and taking feedback.

So take feedback well. And give feedback with grace, knowing that it will inevitably come back to you. And let us all be better because we give and accept healthy feedback better.

Reflection Questions

How good are you at receiving correction from others? _____

_____

Why do you find it difficult to take criticism from some people?

_____

_____

Do you think it's easier to give or take feedback? Why?
_____
_____

How can you prepare yourself to *receive* feedback well, like the "wise person" in Proverbs 9?
_____
_____

How can you improve on *giving* good feedback so the other person receives it well?
_____
_____

Chapter 7: A Predator Called *Imposter*

Matthew 7:13-23

As we approach the end of Jesus' Sermon on the Mount, we find a phrase that was used toward the beginning of His sermon, "enter the Kingdom of Heaven". This phrase and concept function as bookends to His sermon, which is why it is the theme of the message. And as Jesus begins to wind down His sermon, He issues us a warning about imposters...

Matthew 7:13-23,

"Enter through the narrow gate; for the gate is wide and the way is broad that leads to destruction, and there are many who enter through it. [14] For the gate is narrow and the way is constricted that leads to life, and there are few who find it.

[15] "Beware of the false prophets, who come to you in sheep's clothing, but inwardly are ravenous wolves. [16] You will know them by their fruits. Grapes are not gathered from thorn bushes, nor figs from thistles, are they? [17] So every good tree bears good fruit, but the bad tree bears bad fruit. [18] A good tree cannot bear bad fruit, nor can a bad tree bear good fruit. [19] Every tree that does not bear good fruit is cut down and thrown into the fire. [20] So then, you will know them by their fruits.

[21] "Not everyone who says to Me, 'Lord, Lord,' will enter the kingdom of heaven, but the one who does the will of My Father who is in heaven will enter. [22] Many will say to Me on that day, 'Lord, Lord, did we not prophesy in Your name, and in Your name cast out demons, and in Your name perform many miracles?' [23] And then I will declare to them, 'I never knew you; leave Me, you who practice lawlessness.'

In these verses, we see <u>*three things*</u> to avoid. Let's explore them.

False Paths

Jesus describes two radically different directions we can go with our lives: the narrow path or the wide path. We're instructed to choose the narrow path, which is defined by the few who find it, and fewer who seem to choose to walk it, yet leads to life. The broad path, by contrast, seems easy to find, and many will choose that path, even though its end is destruction.

This is the first imposter that wants to seduce us through herd mentality to follow the path most travel. Most of humanity would happily allow others to think for them, rather than do the hard work of considering what is right. What is right is seldom popular, and Jesus teaching us of these two paths highlights this reality.

Isaiah 53:6 tells us of humanity, "All of us, like sheep, have gone astray, **each of us has turned to his own way**; but the Lord has caused the wrongdoing of us all to fall on Him." (emphasis mine). Jesus died and rose again to provide the narrow path that leads to life. But accepting Jesus and walking His path, means surrendering the path we would choose apart from Him. **We cannot love Jesus *and* love the things He died to save us from**. All the attractive, shiny distractions that pull our gaze away from Christ may be sweet and pleasurable now, but the end of them is our own demise.

We must see Jesus as our "Better Yes" even though the narrow path requires dying to self, to be awakened to new life in Christ (Ephesians 2:1-7).

False Prophets

In verses 15-17, we are warned of false prophets, who are compared to wolves in sheep's clothing. It is appropriate to point out here, that Jesus regularly confronts sin in our lives that we would rather not deal with, if not for Him. Walking through this Sermon on the Mount has proven that so far! And any attempt to offer the hope Jesus gives without calling us to die to ourselves (by choosing Jesus' narrow path over mankind's broad path), is a false gospel given by false prophets. They may seem to mean well, but they are drawing people away from the narrow path.

God would never ask someone to deny who they are. That is false! That is exactly what God does. Jesus says in Luke 9, "If anyone wants to come after Me, **he must deny himself**, take up his cross daily, and follow Me. ^{24} For whoever wants to save his life will lose it, but whoever loses his life for My sake, this is the one who will save it. ^{25} For what good does it do a person if he gains the whole world, but loses or forfeits himself?" (Luke 9:23-25, emphasis mine).

The bad news of following Jesus is that you must die to yourself. The good news is that you're already dead spiritually (Ephesians 2:1), so it's not actually forfeiting that much! Leave your "dead" self behind and choose to follow Jesus on the narrow path. And don't buy the dressed-up corpses false prophets are trying to sell on the broad path that leads to destruction.

Of course, "false prophets" are not a new thing. Peter warns against this in 2 Peter 2:1-3, "But false prophets also appeared among the people, just as there will also be false teachers among you, who will secretly introduce destructive heresies, even denying the Master who bought them, bringing swift destruction upon themselves. ^{2} Many will follow their indecent behavior, and because of them the way of the truth will be maligned; ^{3} and in their greed they will exploit you with false words; their judgment from long ago is not idle, and their destruction is not asleep." Peter's warning mirrors that of Jesus: don't be deceived by false prophets who would lead you down their own destructive path.

Jesus *does* love us enough to accept us as we are, but He also loves us too much to leave us that way. We were dead in offenses and sin when He found us. In Him, we're awakened to new life.

False Produce

Lastly, Jesus addresses false produce, or fruit, in verses 17-19. This is in connection to the false prophets, as we are to examine the fruit of their life against the message they proclaim. It is impossible to grow apples from watermelon seeds. The fruit identifies the root. Leaves can be deceiving. The fruit reveals the true character of the branch in question.

The Apostle Paul mirrors this in Galatians 6 where he tells us, "Do not be deceived, God is not mocked; for whatever a person sows, this he will also reap. ⁸ For the one who sows to his own flesh will reap destruction from the flesh, but the one who sows to the Spirit will reap eternal life from the Spirit." (Galatians 6:7-8). Here, we're reminded that what is inside of us will eventually come out. So be mindful of what you and I plant into our lives because we reap what we sow, we reap more than we sow, and we reap later than we sow. Because of this, "Let's not become discouraged in doing good, for in due time we will reap, if we do not become weary." (Galatians 6:9).

My grandparents used to have those bowls of fake fruit in their house. Why do grandparents do that, in the first place?! Anyway, I was about 5 years old and got hungry. So – you guessed it – I grabbed an "apple" from the bowl and bit straight into it! I was immediately disappointed as I spit paint and styrofoam out in confusion and disappointment. False spiritual fruit is the same. It might look "real" on the outside, but it lacks the life and nutrient of the real thing. And in the end, it leaves us spiritually confused and disappointed.

Only life can give life. Unless Jesus has filled us with His life by our faith in Him, it is impossible for us to produce genuine spiritual fruit.

Jesus spoke again about us bearing fruit in John 15:5-6, "I am the vine, you are the branches; the one who remains in Me, and I in him bears much fruit, for apart from Me you can do nothing. ⁶ If anyone does not remain in Me, he is thrown away like a branch and dries up; and they gather them and throw them into the fire, and they are burned." Which leads us right back to Matthew 7…

"Not everyone who says to me, 'Lord, Lord,' will enter the kingdom of heaven, but the one who does the will of my Father who is in heaven. ²² On that day many will say to me, 'Lord, Lord, did we not prophesy in your name, and cast out demons in your name, and do many mighty works in your name?' ²³ And then will I declare to them, 'I never knew you; depart from me, you workers of lawlessness.'" (Matthew 7:21-23).

This is quite an ominous statement by Christ. And it should cause all of us to take pause and examine our relationship with God. He gives three criteria that will not allow us to "enter the Kingdom of Heaven."

- Prophesy (preach) in Jesus' name.
- Cast out demons in Jesus' name.
- Do many mighty works (miracles) in Jesus' name.

What's scary is these sound like preachers! If pastors can't get in, who stands a chance? This echoes the point Jesus made at the beginning of the sermon, that our righteousness must "far surpass" that of the scribes and Pharisees. And if preaching *in Jesus' name*, casting out demons *in Jesus' name*, and even performing miracles *in Jesus' name* is collectively not enough, what's missing?

They never *called* on His name.

I mentioned it earlier, but Romans 10:13 says, "***Everyone* who calls on the name of the Lord *will* be saved**." (emphasis added). The name of Jesus is powerful! At the very name of Jesus, one day every knee will bow, and tongue confess that He is Lord to the glory of God the Father" (Philippians 2:10-11). And one way or another, we will all declare Him as Lord one day. But to enter the Kingdom, we must choose the narrow path, and call upon Him as our Lord and Savior before the Day of Judgment, when all the world will acknowledge Him. So may we choose to surrender to Him here and now, not just as an escape from God's judgment, but out of rightful Lord of all we are.

Reflection Questions

Why does the "broad" way seem so enticing? Why don't more people choose the narrow path?
_____
_____

How do you think we should discern good (yet flawed) pastors, from wolves in sheep's clothing?
_____
_____

Why do you think religious service is not enough to enter the Kingdom of God?
_____
_____

How do you <u>know</u> you will personally enter the Kingdom of Heaven?
_____
_____

Chapter 8: A Promise Called *Security*

Matthew 7:13-23

Welcome to the final chapter of this Bible study on Jesus' Sermon on the Mount! As we wrap up the longest recorded teaching of Jesus, I hope you have found this study helpful in your walk with God. In the last chapter, we discussed the imposters of false *paths*, false *prophets*, and false *produce*. In those verses, Jesus gave us a stern warning that simply knowing about Him is not enough – we must actually follow Him. We need to avoid following imposters that will result in us <u>becoming</u> imposters ourselves.

On the heels of this, Jesus doubles down on the warning, while also reassuring us with the promise that comes from following Him in faith.

Matthew 7:24-28,

"Everyone then who hears these words of mine and does them will be like a wise man who built his house on the rock. ²⁵ And the rain fell, and the floods came, and the winds blew and beat on that house, but it did not fall, because it had been founded on the rock. ²⁶ And everyone who hears these words of mine and does not do them will be like a foolish man who built his house on the sand. ²⁷ And the rain fell, and the floods came, and the winds blew and beat against that house, and it fell, and great was the fall of it." ²⁸ And when Jesus finished these sayings, the crowds were astonished at his teaching, ²⁹ for he was teaching them as one who had authority, and not as their scribes.

Jesus concludes the Sermon on the Mount with a parable of a wise man and a foolish man, and let's take a closer look into this concluding illustration He gives us, that highlights everything He's been teaching in this sermon.

What They Had in Common

Remember that the theme of the Sermon on the Mount **is *entering* and *living* as citizens of the Kingdom**. As He begins this brief parable, He tells us that everyone who *hears* and *does* the things He teaches (i.e., in this sermon), they are like a wise man who built their house upon a rock. He tells us that the foolish person builds a house as well, but they decided that they could just build their house on the sand.

There are a few things they both have in common in the parable – constants, in a science project of sorts. ***The first thing they share is the <u>structure</u> they built***. Like the people in this parable, all of us are building something with our lives. Whether it's a family, a career, something resembling "happiness", or all of the above – there is something you are working toward. The irony is that what you build is not nearly as important as how you build it. For the sake of having a few things in common, Jesus doesn't elaborate on their architecture, general contractor, or style preferences. We're left to understand that the houses are essentially identical in their build aside from their foundation, which we'll get to shortly.

But we learn from this that it doesn't seem to nearly matter _what_ you build with your life, nearly as much as what you build your life _on_. You could become a pastor or a plumber. You could build software to display social media feeds, or you could build feeding centers in a developing country. You could raise a farm or a family... or both. But remember _why_ is always more important than _what_. **Why** you are a pastor, software engineer, plumber, dentist, farmer, stay-at-home mom, etc. is more of a concern of Jesus than the "structure" itself.

The second thing the two builders share is the _storm_. I wish the "wise man" who built his house on the rock was given a pass from the storm. I've lived through hurricanes, tornados, and blizzards with freezing rain. And I haven't enjoyed any of them! Similarly, If you follow Jesus, I can assure you, the very same storms of life will hit you as the person who does not build their life on Christ. Jesus said so, Himself.

In John 16:33, Jesus tells His disciples, "These things I have spoken to you so that in Me you may have peace. In the world you have tribulation, but take courage; I have overcome the world." **Our peace doesn't come from an _absence from the storms_, but from a _presence in the storms_**. He is with us. He is our foundation. Proverbs 10:25, "When the whirlwind passes, the wicked is no more, but the righteous has an everlasting foundation." Several of the psalms in the Old Testament tell us that God is our "refuge" from the storms, our "**very _present_** help in time of need" (Psalm 46:1 emphasis added).

God doesn't deliver us _from_ trouble nearly as often as He delivers us _through_ trouble.

So we can have faith in Him, even in the midst of our storms of life. We may not wish for the trials we have, but only Heaven will be problem-free. And eternity is a lot longer than the troubles we go through now. As Paul would later write, "For our momentary, light affliction is producing for us an eternal weight of glory far beyond all comparison, [18] while we look not at the things which are seen, but at the things which are not seen; for the things which are seen are temporal, but the things which are not seen are eternal." (2 Corinthians 4:17-18).

Where They Differed

The contrast between the two builders is threefold, and just as obvious as the things they had in common. **The first is in their _description_**. We learned in Chapter 6 that a "wise person" can be given instruction, while a "foolish" person cannot (Proverbs 9:7-9). There is a difference between a fool and someone who is ignorant or naïve. The naïve person you can have pity on because they don't know any better. The foolish person, on the other hand, knows better – they just don't care. I've taught our four kids that the famous last words of a fool are, "I know". It takes a wise person to be told there is a better, and to do the wise thing.

The second way the builders differ is in their _decision_. The wise man built his house upon the rock, while the foolish man built his upon the sand. Ephesians 2:19-22, "So then you are no longer strangers and foreigners, but you are fellow citizens with the saints, and are of God's household, ²⁰ having been built on the foundation of the apostles and prophets, Christ Jesus Himself being the cornerstone, ²¹ in whom the whole building, being fitted together, is growing into a holy temple in the Lord, ²² in whom you also are being built together into a dwelling of God in the Spirit." This means that we, collectively are the dwelling of the Holy Spirit and founded upon Jesus and the Word of God. Jesus, the "living Word" (John 1:1-14), is the cornerstone we build everything upon. And like the two paths, everything else will one day meet its end. This leads us to number three...

The final way the builders differ is in their <u>destiny</u>. The wise man's house stood, even though the wind blew against it and "beat on" the house, while the foolish man's house not only fell, but "*great* was the fall of it." While the same exact storm seems to have hit both houses and beat upon them, only the house on the Rock withstood the storm, while the house on the sand was utterly destroyed.

So it is with our lives. If we build our lives upon Jesus and the firm foundation of His commands, we will enter His Kingdom. If we try to go our own way, or build upon anything other than Him, our lives will end in eternal destruction – and great will be the fall of it. This is not an ultimatum, though. If we choose to live our lives apart from Jesus, why would He force us to spend eternity with Him? Our destruction is our choice. Like the foolish man, we should know better. But God will let us build our life upon whatever we wish.

The Crowds were Amazed

As Jesus finished His Sermon on the Mount, the closing description of the crowds' response is that they were "astonished" or amazed at His message. It was said that He spoke "as one who had authority" unlike their scribes. And we should stand in amazement at the person and preaching of Jesus. But we must be more than amazed by Him, we must be changed by Him.

Remember, it was in His concluding parable to this sermon that He says, "Everyone then who *hears* these words of mine and *does* them will be like a wise man..." As James would later write, we must be "*<u>doers</u>* of the Word, and not just <u>*hearers*</u> who deceive themselves." (James 1:22, emphasis mine).

In Closing...

May you *hear* the teachings of Jesus and be diligent to *do* all that He commands. May you find yourself truly blessed as you receive a righteousness not of your own, but that which comes through faith in Christ, and His work *for* you. May His work *through you* be salt and light in a world that desperately needs the difference that He alone can bring. May you grow in community and receive correction from your brothers and sisters in Christ. And may you find your peace in His presence, through every storm of life.

Reflection Questions

What of Jesus' teaching do you need to be a better *doer* in?
_____
_____

How do you respond to God through the storms of life?
_____
_____

What are you going to build upon the Rock?
_____
_____
_____

Memory Verses

Matthew 5:11-12, "Blessed are you when others revile you and persecute you and utter all kinds of evil against you falsely on my account. ¹² Rejoice and be glad, for your reward is great in heaven, for so they persecuted the prophets who were before you."

Matthew 5:13-14, "You are the salt of the earth, but if salt has lost its taste, how shall its saltiness be restored? It is no longer good for anything except to be thrown out and trampled under people's feet. ¹⁴ "You are the light of the world. A city set on a hill cannot be hidden."

Matthew 5:17-18, "Do not think that I have come to abolish the Law or the Prophets; I have not come to abolish them but to fulfill them. ¹⁸ For truly, I say to you, until heaven and earth pass away, not an iota, not a dot, will pass from the Law until all is accomplished."

Matthew 5:20, "For I tell you, unless your righteousness exceeds that of the scribes and Pharisees, you will never enter the kingdom of heaven."

Matthew 5:44, "But I say to you, Love your enemies and pray for those who persecute you."

Matthew 6:1, "Beware of practicing your righteousness before other people in order to be seen by them, for then you will have no reward from your Father who is in heaven."

Matthew 6:9-13, "Pray then like this: "Our Father in heaven, hallowed be your name. ¹⁰ Your kingdom come, Your will be done, on earth as it is in heaven. ¹¹ Give us this day our daily bread, ¹² and forgive us our debts, as we also have forgiven our debtors. ¹³ And lead us not into temptation, but deliver us from evil."

Matthew 6:19-21, "Do not lay up for yourselves treasures on earth, where moth and rust destroy and where thieves break in and steal, ²⁰ but lay up for yourselves treasures in heaven, where neither moth nor rust destroys and where thieves do not break in and steal. ²¹ For where your treasure is, there your heart will be also."

Matthew 6:24, "No one can serve two masters, for either he will hate the one and love the other, or he will be devoted to the one and despise the other. You cannot serve God and money."

Matthew 6:33, "But seek first the kingdom of God and his righteousness, and all these things will be added to you."

Matthew 7:5, "You hypocrite, first take the log out of your own eye, and then you will see clearly to take the speck out of your brother's eye."

Matthew 7:7-8, "Ask, and it will be given to you; seek, and you will find; knock, and it will be opened to you. ⁸ For everyone who asks receives, and the one who seeks finds, and to the one who knocks it will be opened."

Matthew 7:13-14, "Enter by the narrow gate. For the gate is wide and the way is easy that leads to destruction, and those who enter by it are many. ¹⁴ For the gate is narrow and the way is hard that leads to life, and those who find it are few."

Matthew 7:21-23, "Not everyone who says to me, 'Lord, Lord,' will enter the kingdom of heaven, but the one who does the will of my Father who is in heaven. ²² On that day many will say to me, 'Lord, Lord, did we not prophesy in your name, and cast out demons in your name, and do many mighty works in your name?' ²³ And then will I declare to them, 'I never knew you; depart from me, you workers of lawlessness.'"

www.ingramcontent.com/pod-product-compliance
Lightning Source LLC
Chambersburg PA
CBHW080943040426
42444CB00015B/3429